Crystals AND Gems

by Joyce A. Churchill

PEARSON
Scott
Foresman

DK

What You Already Know

Rocks are all around us wherever we live. They are a natural resource of the Earth. Rocks can be large boulders. Sometimes they are broken into small pieces. They can even be finely ground up, like sand.

garnet crystals on a white rock

Over a long time water from rivers and lakes changes rocks. Ice and wind also slowly change rocks and soil. These changes are called erosion and weathering.

Pollution happens when harmful things are put into the environment. We recycle materials to keep the Earth clean and protect its natural resources.

Minerals are natural resources found in rocks. Some kinds of minerals are very special. Most gemstones are special minerals. In this book you will learn how we find gemstones and why we value them.

Crystals and Gems

Minerals are made of atoms. An atom is the tiniest part of all things. Some atoms can come together to make crystals. A crystal is a group of atoms in a pattern, like eggs in an egg crate. Crystals come in different sizes. Rock salt comes in large crystals you can see.

Many gems are also large crystals. Gems that are crystals were formed underground long ago. Volcanoes and earthquakes push them to the surface. When gems reach the surface, people can find them.

Different crystal patterns can grow next to each other.

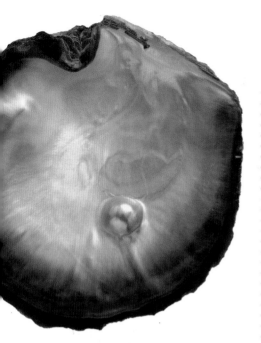

Pearls grow inside
oyster shells.

 pearls

Not all gems come from the Earth. Pearls grow
inside oyster shells. They are shiny and beautiful
when they come from the oyster. Most gemstones
have to be cut by experts.

Gem cutters can make tiny rainbows of light
bounce off a gem. The crystal patterns in the gem
make the light do this.

Diamonds can be found under the ground. People mine diamonds in many countries in the world.

Sometimes miners find diamond ore along rivers in sand and gravel. They use small pans and water to collect diamonds. It takes sharp eyes to tell which stones are the diamonds! Diamond stones have to be sorted, polished, and cut before they can become gems.

a diamond mine in South Africa

The diamonds in this pan are not cut or polished.

Gems can be precious or semiprecious. Gems that are hard to find or collect are called precious. Gems that are easier to find are called semiprecious.

Scientists can also make synthetic gems. These are copies that look like real gems. Scientists grow crystals in a special container. Then they heat and apply pressure to the crystals. People buy synthetic gems because they cost less than real ones.

Synthetic gems look just like real gems.

synthetic ruby crystal

synthetic cut ruby

How hard are minerals?

Minerals can be hard or soft. Chalk is a soft mineral. You can scratch chalk with your fingernail and leave a mark. Soft minerals break into pieces. Their atoms link lightly together.

Diamonds are the hardest mineral. They have atoms made of carbon. The atoms in a diamond link together like a tight web. A diamond is strong enough to cut through other rocks. People use diamonds in cutting tools.

The Mohs scale shows how hard minerals are.

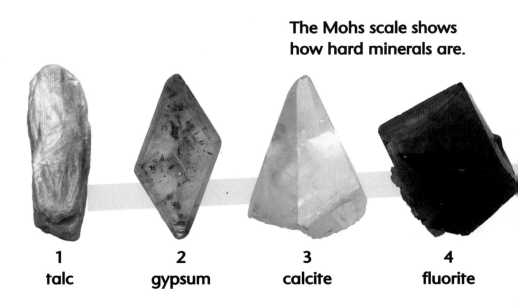

1	2	3	4
talc	gypsum	calcite	fluorite

Frederick Mohs was a scientist from Germany. In 1822 he found a way to show how hard different minerals are. He gave minerals different numbers depending on their hardness. This is called the Mohs scale.

Look at the scale below. Soft minerals have low numbers. Talc is very soft. It is number 1 on the scale. Hard minerals get high numbers. Diamonds are number 10.

10
diamond

9
corundum

8
topaz

5
apatite

6
feldspar

7
quartz

This rock from a volcano has a diamond in it.

diamond ring

Diamond

Diamonds were formed deep in the Earth many years ago. Diamonds need to be dug or blasted out of the ground. One of the most famous diamond mines is in South Africa.

Diamond ore is loaded into trucks and taken to a crusher. Crushed ore is then taken to be washed. Diamonds are separated from the waste material. The diamonds are sorted into five thousand different kinds! They are sorted by size, shape, color, and value.

Most diamonds are clear, like glass. Some can be light yellow. Light reflects through the patterns of their crystals. That is why diamonds sparkle. Most diamonds have facets like a baseball diamond cut into them.

Quartz

Quartz can be found in small streams, in rivers, and on beaches. Quartz is made of crystals and is quite hard. Many semiprecious gems are made from quartz.

Quartz can be transparent. This means you can see through it, like water. Some quartz is opaque. This means you can't see through it at all, like milk.

There are many kinds of quartz. Amethyst quartz is purple. Citrine quartz comes in shades of transparent orange. Rose quartz is pink.

quartz beads

Amethyst is a type of quartz. Can you see the patterns of the crystals?

Ruby

Rubies come in all shades of red. They are precious gemstones. Kings and queens in Europe used rubies in their crowns. Rubies are cut from a mineral called corundum. It is very hard but not as hard as a diamond.

Rubies come from mines in Asia and Africa. Some countries where they are found are Myanmar, Sri Lanka, and Thailand.

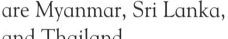

cut ruby

The Edwardes Ruby is so large it is kept in a museum.

Can you see the star in this sapphire?

sapphire in rock

Sapphire

Sapphires are precious gems. They can be pale blue or almost black. Sapphires are a hard, transparent stone. Just like rubies, they are made of corundum.

Sapphires are found in Asia. They are mined in Thailand, India, Sri Lanka, and Myanmar. They are also found in Australia. In the United States sapphires have been found in the state of Montana.

Opal

Opals are made up of tiny spheres. A sphere is a shape like a ball.

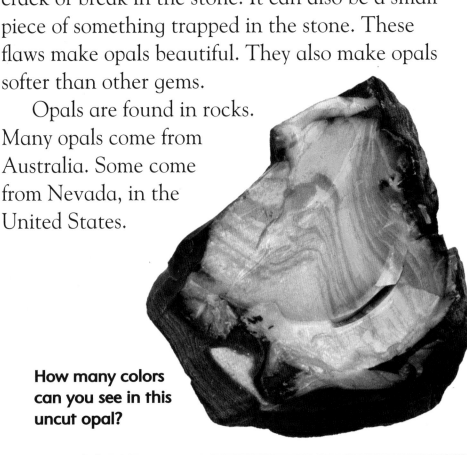

dark opal pendant

One opal stone can be red, green, blue, and yellow. The colors in an opal come from flaws. A flaw is a little crack or break in the stone. It can also be a small piece of something trapped in the stone. These flaws make opals beautiful. They also make opals softer than other gems.

Opals are found in rocks. Many opals come from Australia. Some come from Nevada, in the United States.

How many colors can you see in this uncut opal?

Emerald

Emeralds are precious gems. They are made of a mineral called beryl. It is a hard mineral with layers of crystals.

Emeralds have been valued for thousands of years. The ancient Egyptians mined emeralds and used them to make jewelry. The finest emeralds today are found in the country of Colombia, in South America. They have been mined there for more than four hundred years.

polished emerald

cut emerald

The top of this crystal is a green emerald.

Topaz

Another gemstone made from tiny crystals is topaz. It comes in many pale colors. Topaz can be brown, blue, or green. Some topaz is red. It can also be colorless.

Topaz is a hard mineral. It can be cut into many interesting shapes. Topaz is a semiprecious gem. It is often used for rings and other jewelry.

Topaz is found in Russia, Brazil, and Australia. It is also mined in Mexico and the United States.

topaz ring

This topaz has many flaws at the bottom.

Uncut moonstone reflects silver, blue, and orange.

Moonstone

When light reflects off moonstone, it glows like light from the Moon. Moonstone is made from a mineral called feldspar. Half of all the rocks on Earth are made of feldspar.

Moonstones are found in several countries. Many are mined in Sri Lanka and Tanzania. They are also found in the United States.

moonstone necklace

Tree sap was a soft, sticky trap for this insect. The sap turned into hard amber.

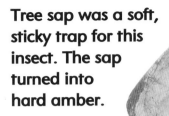

Amber

Amber is different from many other gems. It is not made of crystals. Amber is made of resin, or sap, from ancient trees. Soft tree resin takes millions of years to turn into hard amber. Most amber is yellow or brown. Amber can also be red, green, or blue.

A piece of amber is very light. It is often transparent. You can sometimes see insects, leaves, or moss trapped inside. Scientists study animals and plants trapped in amber to learn about life long ago.

amber beads

Jet

Jet is also different from many other gems. It is sometimes called black amber. Jet is not made from crystals. It comes from ancient plant parts. Some jet used to be wood! Millions of years of pressure under the Earth changed the wood into a black mineral. Like amber, jet can be easily polished.

Jet is mined in Spain, France, and Germany. It is also found in Russia and the United States. Shiny, black stones in jewelry are often pieces of jet.

jet earrings

Look for the wood grain in this piece of jet.

Special Gems

Gemstones have been special for thousands of years. Long ago, kings and queens wore precious gems in their crowns. Pirates sometimes raided ships to steal the jewels. Many early peoples buried their rulers along with precious gems. Today, you can see the jewels from their tombs in many museums.

People in the past thought gems could help them. Emeralds were worn to protect people from animal bites. Topaz was thought to bring friends. Rubies were worn to protect people from feeling sad.

Many people still like to give gemstones as gifts for special celebrations. In many countries in the world, people give each other a ring with a gemstone when they get married. People also give gemstones as birthday gifts. Did you know there is a special list of gemstones for each month of the year? These are called birthstones.

December turquoise

January garnet

February amethyst

November topaz

March aquamarine

October opal

Which of these birthstones matches your birthday month?

April diamond

September sapphire

May emerald

August peridot

June pearl

July ruby

Our Hidden Treasure

amber

Rocks are made up of minerals. Minerals are found all over the Earth.

Gemstones are a special group of minerals. Many come from deep in the Earth. Some have been pushed up to the surface of the Earth by volcanoes.

Gemstones are taken out of rocks through mining. They are washed and polished. Facets are cut into them so that they can reflect light from their crystal patterns.

sapphire

Proustite is a crystal mineral that is purple like amethyst.

Gemstones that are rare are called precious stones. Those that are more easily found are called semiprecious stones.

People have valued gemstones for thousands of years. They are some of our most beautiful natural resources.

amethyst

Glossary

atoms   the smallest parts of all things

crystal   a group of atoms in a pattern

facets   sides cut into a gemstone

opaque   something you cannot see through, like milk

precious   the most rare and valuable gemstones

semiprecious   the less rare and less valuable gemstones

synthetic   something made by people and machines

transparent   clear, see-through